LOST IN TRANSLATION

LOST IN TRANSLATION

A COLLECTION OF RECORDED POEMS AND EMOTIONS

ASTRORA

To Walter Sperling,
My Dad.
Happy Birthday!
This one's for you.
12/1/2021

IF THIS BOOK HAS MADE ITS WAY INTO YOUR
FRAGILE HANDS,
I COULDN'T BE HAPPIER
IF THIS SORT OF THING MAKES YOU SMILE,
BY ALL MEANS CONSIDER IT ALL YOURS
LIFE IS FULL OF SO MANY LITTLE MOMENTS,
AND QUITE A FEW BIG ONES, TOO
MOMENTS IN BETWEEN THOSE ARE MADE
OF MAGIC—
OF THAT MUCH, I AM SURE.
ONE THING I'D LIKE TO ASK OF YOU MOVING
FORWARD INTO FOREVER IS—
TO ALWAYS REACH INSIDE YOURSELF,
AND
TO ALWAYS EMBRACE THE MOMENT
WHAT IS IN THE *HERE* AND *NOW*
AND WHEN YOU CAN'T FATHOM TO REACH,
OR WHEN ITS TOO DIFFICULT TO EMBRACE
WHEN THE MOMENT IS A BIT SCARY AND
FRIGHTENING TO FACE
I ONLY WISH THAT YOU CHOOSE TO ALWAYS
TRY AND FIND FAITH
TO ALWAYS TAKE A CHANCE,
CHOOSE TO ALWAYS,

BE **BRAVE**

XS

ON LOVE

AS DEEP

AS

THE COSMOS

WHEN FOOLS FALL IN LOVE

It never fails to mystify me,
How raindrops falling from the windowpanes
Falling in droplets
Reminds me
Of falling in love
How I felt
When I first learned your name
It never fails to mystify me
How fire first flickers before
Growing into a flame
Burning fast
A fire's love lasts
Only as quickly as it came
I flickered
When I first learned your name
It never fails to mystify me
How seeing you
Was like seeing
Delicate snow falling
For the very first time
Slowly, then surely,
Then glowing, all at once.

It isn't hard to write about you. Fools in love would agree,
what you love should come easy.

What do you say you and I make a bet:
You win, I'm a fool for you.
I win, I'm a fool for you.
Either way, I don't reckon either of us are in favor of losing.

UNIVERSE IN RELATION

There exists
A universe in relation
In the distance
Between Me
And You

The way your heart aches
and even in some of the ways that it breaks
It emits miles of cosmic energy that,
if not careful,
Can split even Jupiter in two.

See, when your heart *aches*,
It dwells in its own variations of Blue.
I tend to believe,
Your heart can be as blue as Neptune.

There exists in this reality
A dimension of alternate choices and celestial possibilities
Swift and subtle shooting stars full of golden opportunities
There is a plethora of gizmos that battle between the
if I do's and *if I don'ts*
Each seemingly centuries away as we travel further
down this telescope
that is full of wonder that in this moment if expanded
would reach the sun
And when I think of that wonder—well nothing on this whole
planet could possibly outnumber
The one thing in existence
that keeps *you*
stranded *here*
on earth
with *me*
and,
Even though you tend to live in the structure of that galaxy in
your mind
The one thing you have that creation in full has been envying you
since the beginning of time begins with;

The way you hold the secrets of the cosmos
The way you hold your tongue,
And the way your eyes are like the dark side
of the moon,
The way you inhale stardust that inflates your
lungs
Yes,
You are a black **hole**
Your mysterious energy is undefined and to be
cautioned with, *reckoned* with
Messing around with you temperamentally,
could accidentally
be the cause of the whole Big Bang
In theory;

And the concept of time,
Is so in love with you.
The showers of meteors come Racing. After. You.
For you,
Spirals of pastel neons and electric fire dance for you
If only just to keep you breathing and
Alive

There exists
A Universe in Relation
In the distance
Between Me
And You—

There is more than myself, and more than anyone else
in this pixel of existence
But none of that even matters
because there still exists this universe between us
the universe you are made of
everything you are compelled by
your gravitational defenses weighing everything down
nothing could every reach you
no amounts of helium could navigate me close enough to even try,
no
I wouldn't even break the atmosphere

But for you,
robustly
In an extraterrestrial, complex, and destructive matter
For you,
in an array of ultraviolet colors
I would die—just to try
Because there exists
A Universe in Relation
In the distance Between Me,
And You

Your touch lingers like stardust
Falling infinitely into a black hole.
Aching and dwelling, forever.

You are a ray of sun
You set my soul on fire
To the point where I, too,
Begin to glimmer and shine.

I'm almost certain you are it.
The first thing I'd reach for
if it meant coming back to everything
I've ever known.
You are my home.

AND THE WORDS

And when I look at you
I'm reminded of a place I once visited,
a place I once visited among the moon
I'm reminded of the moment we met
How your eyes were like falling sunsets
How I dove deep into their dark wet pools and how I instantly
knew I would let you
Become the energy source of my soul
That's right. The energy source of my soul. And you did.
How you embraced the depth of my shallow vessel and put
weight into my body, fueling the engines inside me that would
Condescendingly catch fire within my veins
You started my engines and then it began
The speed of emotion against time and space,
You were the start of my engine again and again and again
Until at last my rocket took aim, and fired through the dense
Milky Way
Getting lost in the comets of glistening way I regained both my
steering and piloting strength and landed on the moon
And it was weightless from there.
Tasting you was like being on that glowing, desolate rock:
it was effortless and gorgeous
It was quiet like Saturn's secrets
And honestly, the view of earth was not bad from up there

Floating in circles for you, I could
Create new craters on the moon, I could
Build you a constellation, I could
If you would've let me I could,
Have given you the galaxy—just as you had given me the gift of
sending me to the moon with all of only the depths of your eyes
And when you *blinked* how the whole solar system shook
When you *blinked* how the stars themselves came tumbling down
The sun had caught fire and Neptune had drowned
The moon lost its power and craters collided
To break down the rocket in which I had
confided
In you
And how it took but all of gravity
To send me tumbling back down to earth
In the heaviest of ways
And the words escape me
At all altitudes did I learn, how I, too, was capable
Of committing one giant leap for mankind
Only love, in the blink of an eye
Can make you do something crazy like that.

Do you see, how after all this time
It was time itself that saved you for me?
Love was not lost.

And then he kissed her.
Desperately, deliberately.

He knew what doing this meant, but it didn't matter.
Because he also knew only one thing
was important in that moment:
The relief in translating the *obvious* truth.

FOREVER AND EVER AND EVER

I'll flock to you
Until the turn of the sun setting reflects
the dark side of the moon,
until the stars fall like raindrops
Falling into the palms of your hands,
Until the irrational affirmation that
I don't— becomes I can—
Do anything—absolutely everything
That your wildest dreams desire
I'll chase that fire
Until there is no more til. Until the end of time.
I will ride the tide of how high it makes me feel
Whenever you and I lock eyes
I want to shower the cosmic radiation that falls
in admiration overneath our night sky
I want that shower of sequestration
radiating dewdrops of jubilation
to fall from the tear ducts of your eyes I—
want so very badly, just to see you shine

Would you have ever reckoned,
That a hopeless romantic like me
Would shamelessly stand here,
My chest naked in all honesty
At the rawness of a black hole that has been made full
By the likings of someone like you?

Would you ever have reckoned,
That a dollop of you echoing laughter
Would have followed me throughout the cosmos?
Because I'd have reckoned, that you had me strung around the
ring of your lasso
Swinging around and around and around
There is no end limit to how much I'd linger
Tied to your lasso for as long as you'd let me
Constant in our together
And I will adore you
Forever and ever and ever
Until there is no more til. Until the end of time.

PARIS

"Paris would be good for you," he says.
"Why Paris?" I ask.
"The coffee, art, poetry, rebellion, muggy weather, fun hats;
you should go."
"Paris then...I'd love to."
"I'll meet you if you do."
"Would you really?"
"I decided, yes."
"Why is that?"
"Because you, like Paris, really blossom in the Spring."

romance

I started falling in love with him
a little like rain started falling
slowly in droplets
and then pouring down heavy
Nobody teaches you on how to bear the storm
Nobody teaches you
on how to steady your own heartbeat at the mention of their
name
your veins pulsing with electricity
a certain flame burning from your insides
making itself known that in the quiet moments between deciding
to take a leap or choosing to stand still
You take a deep breath because you're afraid to find out
but still you must ask
"What comes next?"
"What is happening to me?"

You're the kind of girl people write poetry about
A living, breathing piece of art
That only certain people
Can scarcely fathom to put into words.

Poets falling in love with Poets
are such a bittersweet thing—
On one hand, the ebbing and flowing of words
that spiral forever
On the other, a chaotic and beautiful kind of
timeless.

It's almost *chemical*,
The reaction(s) I feel for you.

You are a chrome heart
Unstable in oxygen
Hard to the touch
Impossible to rust
But you also shine
You also glimmer
Though you tarnish,
You are still resistant
You are an outer shell of your most inner
Endlessly defending yourself
You are a chrome heart
Stubborn in your chemical properties
From your metal to your dust
You do more than just luster
You exist to shine

Something in you is *somewhere*,
Dwelling in your blood as you question, as you search,
As you subconsciously put yourself on the path to fill the empty
voids, the missing part.

And everything in me is going to find you.

And what more can we say now?
After all is said and done,
Isn't it love that still remains?

This is a speechless discovery
Echoing from the heart.

And I don't know what your opinion on this is.
You might not feel the same, and perhaps it's best that you don't.
Best that you don't reach out to me. Best that you don't respond
to our conversations anymore. Best that you leave me alone,
so I can leave you alone.
Best not to explore the option. Best not to seize the chance.
It would be best, so I don't have to write this open letter like this.
Because if you do react—if you were to admit there is *something*
magnetizing you and I together—
Something you can't quite put into words just as I can't
Something that seems all too familiar but you're unable to define
just as I can't
Well...
Then I'm not sure what to make of that
Because so much in me is translating to the possibility
of just one word;

Fate.

ON SADNESS

THAT DWELLS

AS DEEP

AS A

BLACKHOLE

How sad and true it is,
That you harbor everything you have been through.
Some of those things just mold onto the armor.

Listen to me: you are not defined by what hurt you.
Defining grounds are drawn by where you choose to stand.
Definition is a *choice*.

LASSO

I will wait
however long it takes
for you to
travel back to me from across the galaxy where you are;
because you promised
And I will wait
with an open door and a light on
to welcome you back partner
to welcome you back into the warmth of my arms
and into the strong pull of all the cosmic words
that I have gathered over the ages
just to make you feel at home again
here
on *Earth*
with *me*
and
I will hold you as you unwind your biological clock
and settle into the fine moment lingering
I will watch you with detailed observation as the vibration of
your laughter
fills the spaces that were empty
just moments before you had came,
if I'm being honest, it fills me up just the same
Because *God only knows*
how I was *tested*, I'll say

while I sat in my chair and waited for you
rocking back and forth, yes
God only knows the trials and tribulations I had overcome
as I peered out my little telescope and searched across the nebulas
for you
And as I looked and looked yonder outside my window for
you
restricted by gravity and the hinged frame that
bounded me and held me hostage inside
when all I wanted was to hold you;
I wished and wished and wished with all of my soul
that the stars you were among would send you
rocketing back to me
and
Even if not right away
Even if not today
I would have continued to wait.
There are so many words I could sputter
to describe the length of time
I am willing to sit and patiently rock back and forth anticipating
your arrival with
but words can't define the reasoning instilled in my ways
Because nothing comes close to defining the lining in
the fragile fragments that in many forms of pixilation
make up the depth between you and me
Nothing comes close to everything we've been through
Everything we've battled and won claim over
With baton in hand and shield in the other
Nothing compares to our story
Written among the series of constellations
We exceeded the expectations
and set the new standard,
You and I, We

are the new modern day tweed-stitched
highest degree in certainty,
of what a history in romantics has struggled to define
what the rotation of the planet cannot fathom to try to hide
and what even you my space cowboy on your dark horse race to
find
As I remember quite clearly when you kissed me,
you told me not to cry
We share a Universe in Relation that became when you lassoed
away
and left me with your blinding light that transported you
to the starting of the drawn out milky way
And before you teleported into the dimensional portal
that would send you a billion light years away from me,
You promised me a safe arrival
You promised me you'd never forget
how could you forget,
that you were with me now and forever
through all of space and time?
And as trillions and tons of brilliant lights passed us
like a madman space cowboy,
oh how you cupped my face in your hands,
you looked me straight in the eye as you leaned in to tell me
"you will be alright."
And before I could respond you said
"I'll be back for you,"
while holding onto your worn western hat
as I remember the forces of a black hole spinning and sucking
your lasso into its endless mouth, preparing itself to propel you
into the vastness of space

"I promise"
you said as I cried at your departure, the hurling and zipping and
zapping dissolving you into a million tiny pieces
before a clap of thunder slang you on your robotic dark horse
becoming but a distant star among the many I see in the now
night sky

"Don't cry,"
your voice echoed,
over and over more faintly every time
as I looked for you but couldn't see you
"I'll be back for you,"
It continues for days and days forever
"I promise,"
I hear you in a frenzy
around every corner,
every bend,
every day,
your promise remains

And I hold to that quite faithfully
with just my telescope beside me
as I wait for the stars to come out every night

And I will sit in my little chair
and I will wait
however long it takes.

And ours was a hard love.
A steadfast, but utterly complicated love.
And in the end, was what gave you away.
I think about you here and then.

Somebody has to say it, and I'll be damned if it's not me:
You're worth it.
Infinite times.
Every time.

Artificial love cannot be made.
It simply isn't real.

I am all sorts of *crooked;*
I bend in all creases of the word.

He and I were a constance that would never work
Attracted to each other's outstanding opposite nature
It was irony
He was as detached and empty as a black hole
I was a radiating sun that he couldn't swallow to comprehend
I was too warm, too inviting, too much for him to feel
So much that when my light reached—
It couldn't escape within him

So much that when he tried—
His own gravity drowned just to feel my flames

"be fragile with me," she said.
"why?"
"I was too delicate then, and I wasn't handled with care."
She had no idea how impressive she was
A flower learning to use her thorns
Still bursting with color
Still learning to bloom
Still just as sweet

For the majority—
love was one of those things she just didn't make time for.
She couldn't help but think that time—very much like life—
was too vast, too infinite, to squeeze in something
like love that was so *small*. That was *constant*.
Something that *varied*.
Something that required a consistent attention in the case that it
should *leave*.

"But how can energy pass like that?" She asks me.
"How does cosmic energy transfer away from the dust we are
made of,
and leave us aching for more?"
Tears form in her eyes, the heavy pull of a wet sigh escaping
her,
wet plops falling to her cheeks and then sinking to her shirt,
staining her in drying drips of salt.
Her chest shudders as a sharp cry escapes through the grit of
her teeth.
"How can it leave you with such a black hole?"
She shakes.
"That is just *so, so* cruel."

In your mind is such a messy place to be.

How do you define the disconnect?
Where does your mind go?
Why on *earth* can't I go with you?

Lonely people are the most misunderstood.

There is so much you say between the lines when you talk.
None of which measures up to how you actually feel.

BURNING SKY

If the world was burning
There's no one else I'd rather watch it burn with than you
And I'm stupid for not saying it before
The chaos didn't come when you left
No, the chaos came crashing in pieces in everything that stayed
replaying endlessly in my head:
Every conversation
Every laugh
Every silent thought passing between us
Achingly falling apart at the seams the more I looked back
again and again and again
For me it never ends
I find it rather revolutionary
The way we complement each other
Two forces of nature that *if* needless to say
We should find ourselves
in the most extraordinary of circumstances
Should the world be burning
In a falling firestorm of fury
In the ashes and the dust
Searching through the embers the only thing more chaotic
Would be if I wasted it away without the chance to tell you
What I feared before and what I fear too late now
That if you were here beside me
Your eyes in mine
Two sets of holes endlessly falling into each other

Your hands in mine
Locked ferociously, devotedly
With the wind howling and cutting away pieces of heat
dissolving into the stinging pores of our skin
With the wilting air leaving you and I both *gasping*
Your lips desperately, hungrily
Melting into mine
We share our oxygen
In an effort to save time
As the final elements began to combust and release
The end of the earth, the end of all time, the end of everything
as we knew it
And the sky,
was set in the last ultimate showdown
a never setting sun
A revolutionary burning sky
Trapping us in its bittersweet inferno
The furious complication of having you
but having you too late
Moments lost in the sea of time undoing
As the reality we knew furnaced to its end
And I, with the last of life I could comprehend
Would choose to spend it with you
Because that was the kind of enough
It's you I'd watch it burn in flames with
Because you were always the one

"Don't fall in love with me," she cautioned—her words pulsing
in my veins.
"Loving a poet is dangerous. Because even after the sun rises, it
almost still always rains."

Sometimes, you wish you can take away the pain other
people are feeling, you know?
Kind of like you are doing with me right now. But we can't.
We must feel things.
And pain, like most things, is one of those things we have to grow
through. It must be felt. It is a sentiment of the heart.
It is a testament of being *alive*.

Don't linger. You know how that makes you feel.
Respect yourself enough to push through.

Do it for yourself.

Don't linger. Move forward.
Don't stop now.
You've already come this far.

ON THE AFFIRMATION

THAT YOU, TOO,

ARE RELATIVE

TO THE UNIVERSE

Some days I feel like the winner.
Other days I harbor the loss.
Mostly I forget I'm still playing the game.

She drank her wine with gusto—the life of what she was
Sparkling right back in her eyes
With every sip from the bottle
Bubbles of joy and the essence of light
Escaping her lips
Cracking at the taste
Vida

There's a fine but distinct difference,
Between being lonely and being alone.
If you ever find yourself in your lonesome, know I'm here.
Promise me when the lonely hour finds you, you'll call me.
Please, don't forget to call.

A gentle mind comes from a peaceful heart.

How clever. Your actions mask every word you cannot say.
Who hurt you? When will you finally let it go?

Do you ever ask the stars
if they can see you twinkling too?

You are your own seed
Waiting to blossom, waiting to emerge
Water, sun, breathe, repeat
Bloom
You will bloom

I am a poet;
Words dwelling in a body
Aching to be set free

If you knew a lick about me, there'd be no guessing what my
intentions are.
The real ones know heart is a dangerous thing,
but used correctly—
and you become the defender of those it speaks for.

Do you think we'll make it far out there?
Do you suppose there's whiskey waiting as the congratulatory
prize?

She was hard to love.
But with that *pressure*
came the diamond hidden on the inside.

It's a brave thing to make the first move.
You're not guaranteed it will or won't be your last.

I dare you to always go first anyways.

Love, and let love.
For your own sake.
Love has *always* been the answer.

Try to always stay close to people
who always make you feel warm.
You deserve to stay happy.
Warm people tend to already know this truth.

It was a thunderous thing,
The lightning in her heart.

I pray for all the vulnerable people
who have exposed their soft self
to the eyes of those
who have turned the other way

It takes a certain kind of courage
to reveal the heart
and not all who have seen
are capable of such beauty
not all who have seen
are deserving of such things

The world does not stand still
It goes through various turns and changes
And so must you

When the echoes say you are not enough,
Find the courage to say otherwise
You have a voice and it is

Beautiful

It's very possible to fall as much into the sky
as it is to fall into your mind and heart
when you miss someone you love

The depth is endless
and sometimes all you can do
Is look up
and relate

Love is a force so strong
It echoes in all forms
From the past to the present and future
Making itself known
Some things do not need saying
As much more as they need to be felt
Some things need not be seen physically
To know the feeling is still there
Echoing forever

Love finds you wherever you are

One simple truth:

If you find the light in everything,
You become the light.

Sarah Sperling, poetically known as Astrora, is a writer/poet based out of Orlando, Florida.She prefers the overcast days of rain to that of sun, and enjoys reading under candlelight accompanied by her black cat, Pluto.

Publishing at 30 years old, *Lost In Translation* is her debut collection of poetry inspired by many sunsets, many people, many moments taken and crafted into the making of this book. In the many hopes, and attempts, that it would reach someone exactly like you.

Astrora and her work can be found by visiting www.booksbyastrora.com and on Instagram at @astrora_